HAL•LEONARD
INSTRUMENTAL
PLAY-ALONG

CLASSICAL SOLOS
FOR
TENOR SAXOPHONE
VOLUME 2

ONLINE MEDIA INCLUDED
Audio Recordings
Printable Piano Accompaniments

PLAYBACK+
Speed • Pitch • Balance • Loop

T0081581

To access recordings and PDF accompaniments, visit:
www.halleonard.com/mylibrary

Enter Code
6341-0722-8905-4241

ISBN 978-1-4803-5120-2

HAL•LEONARD®

Visit Hal Leonard Online at
www.halleonard.com

In Europe, contact:
Hal Leonard Europe Limited
42 Wigmore Street
Marylebone, London, W1U 2RN
Email: info@halleonardeurope.com

LARGO
from *Xerxes*

GEORGE FRIDERIC HANDEL
Arranged by PHILIP SPARKE

B♭ TENOR SAXOPHONE

Largo (♩ = 68)

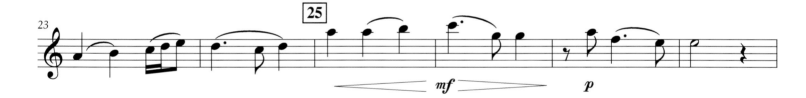

Slower

SONGS MY MOTHER TAUGHT ME

from *Gypsy Songs*

ANTONÍN DVORÁK
Arranged by PHILIP SPARKE

B♭ **TENOR SAXOPHONE**

Andante con moto
(♩ = 108)

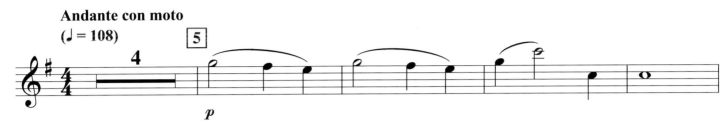

00121141

3

MINUET NO. 2
from *Notebook for Anna Magdalena Bach*

B♭ TENOR SAXOPHONE

Attributed to CHRISTIAN PEZOLD
Arranged by PHILIP SPARKE

00121141

LA CINQUANTAINE
from *Two Pieces for Cello and Piano*

Bᵇ TENOR SAXOPHONE

JEAN GABRIEL-MARIE
Arranged by PHILIP SPARKE

SEE, THE CONQUERING HERO COMES

from *Judas Maccabeus*

Bb TENOR SAXOPHONE

GEORGE FRIDERIC HANDEL
Arranged by PHILIP SPARKE

Allegro (♩ = 132)

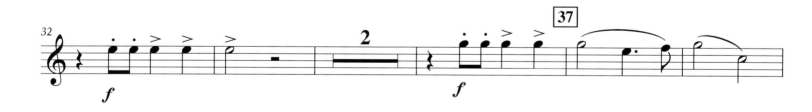

rall.

00121141

SONATINA
Op. 36, No. 1

MUZIO CLEMENTI
Arranged by PHILIP SPARKE

B♭ TENOR SAXOPHONE

00121141

7

SERENATA
from *String Quartet, Op. 3, No. 5*

FRANZ JOSEPH HAYDN
Arranged by PHILIP SPARKE

B♭ TENOR SAXOPHONE

Andante cantabile (♩ = 96)

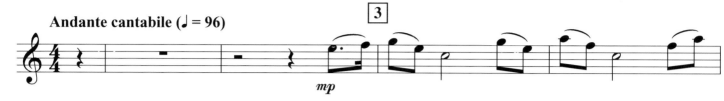

TAMBOURIN
from *Second Suite in E Minor*

B♭ TENOR SAXOPHONE

JEAN-PHILIPPE RAMEAU
Arranged by PHILIP SPARKE

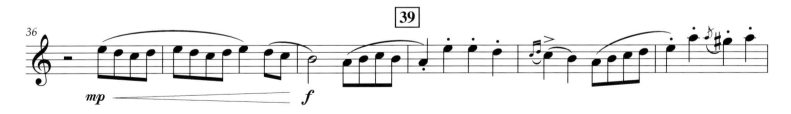

00121141

WALTZ
from *Album for the Young*

PYOTR ILYICH TCHAIKOVSKY
Arranged by PHILIP SPARKE

B♭ TENOR SAXOPHONE

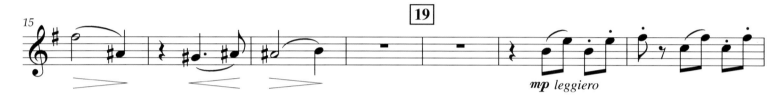

SONATINA
from *Six Pieces, Op. 3*

CARL MARIA VON WEBER
Arranged by PHILIP SPARKE

B♭ TENOR SAXOPHONE

Moderato e con amore
(♩ = 120)

GAVOTTE
from *Paride ed Elena*

CHRISTOPH GLUCK/arr. JOHANNES BRAHMS
Arranged by PHILIP SPARKE

B♭ TENOR SAXOPHONE

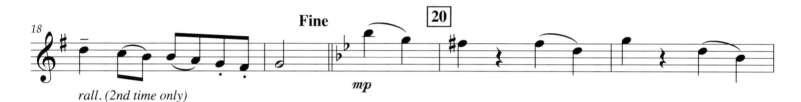

SONATA
Op. 118, No. 1

ROBERT SCHUMANN
Arranged by PHILIP SPARKE

B♭ TENOR SAXOPHONE

Moderato
(♩ = 104)

SERENADE
from *Schwanengesang, D.957*

FRANZ SCHUBERT
Arranged by PHILIP SPARKE

Bb TENOR SAXOPHONE

Andante con moto
(♩ = 84)

SONATINA
Anh. 5, No. 1

B♭ TENOR SAXOPHONE

LUDWIG VAN BEETHOVEN
Arranged by PHILIP SPARKE

Moderato
(♩ = 126)

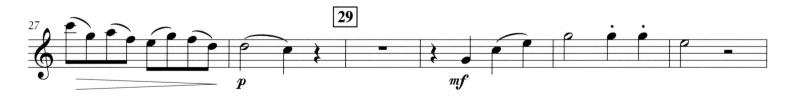

00121141

BOURRÉE
from *Flute Sonata, HWV 363b*

GEORGE FRIDERIC HANDEL
Arranged by PHILIP SPARKE

B♭ TENOR SAXOPHONE